Simple
Stir-fries

Your Promise of Success

Welcome to the world of Confident Cooking, created for you in our
test kitchen, where recipes are double-tested by our team of home
economists to achieve a high standard of success.

PERIPLUS

Seasoning your wok

New carbon steel woks must always be cleaned and seasoned before use. This removes the protective film which coats them when they are sold and which prevents them from rusting. Stainless steel, cast-iron and non-stick woks don't need to be seasoned.

Add 2 tablespoons of bicarbonate of soda to a wok full of cold water and bring it to a rapid boil for 15 minutes. Discard the water, then scrub off the coating with a scourer, repeating the process if required. Rinse and dry thoroughly. Place the wok over high heat and use paper towels to wipe peanut or vegetable oil over the inner surface. Repeat until the paper towels come away clean. Reduce the heat to low and leave the wok for about 15 minutes to absorb the oil. Repeat the oiling process before using the wok for the first time. The coating will build up over time and provide a desirable, non-stick finish.

Cast-iron, stainless steel or non-stick woks need no special cleaning treatment. To clean a carbon steel wok, allow it to cool, then wash it with hot water, using a soft brush or cloth.

Ensure that it is thoroughly dry and wipe the inside with a thin layer of oil before storing. The inside of a properly seasoned carbon steel wok should not be scrubbed. Avoid using detergent unless it is absolutely necessary, as they will damage the seasoning. If you do need to use detergent or steel wool to clean your wok, it will need to be re-seasoned before storing.

Stir-frying

Stir-frying involves the quick cooking of small pieces of food over high heat using minimal oil. The characteristic action of stir-frying is to toss the food constantly with a shovel-like utensil called a 'charn' — a spade-like scoop that is ideal for the continuous, fast scooping and turning motion required.

Stir-frying is regarded as a healthy cooking method, with good reason. The rapid cooking time preserves many of the food's nutrients with most of the colour and vitamins intact. Because properly seasoned woks develop a non-stick coating, very little oil is needed when stir-frying. Ensure the oil has a mild flavour so that the flavour of your ingredients aren't masked

New carbon steel woks are coated in a thin oily lacquer to prevent them from rusting before they are brought home.

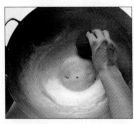

Once you have boiled the water and bicarbonate of soda in the wok, make sure you scrub every bit of the coating off.

To season the wok, put it over high heat. Dip paper towels in oil and wipe over the inner surface of the wok.

should also have a high burning point so it can be safely heated to the high temperatures required.

The secret to successful stir-frying is to remember that once you begin, you must keep going. There is no time to interrupt the cooking process to chop an ingredient or mix a sauce. All ingredients to be stir-fried should be prepared before you even heat the wok. When you heat the wok, you need to ensure that the heat is intense enough to sear the food and seal in any juices so that they don't stew.

When preparing stir-fry ingredients, cut them into small, even pieces, so they cook rapidly and evenly. Meat or poultry should be sliced into thin, uniform-sized slices across the grain — you will find that slicing is easier if the meat is frozen for about 30 minutes beforehand, however never refreeze meat that has been defrosted. When cooking large quantities of meat, cook it in small batches to avoid stewing the food in its own juices.

Long vegetables, such as leafy stems, asparagus and green beans are cut on the diagonal, to increase their surface area, thereby hastening the cooking time. If the vegetables have been washed, they should be dried thoroughly so that they don't add too much moisture to the mixture.

Glossary of ingredients

bok choy

(Chinese chard, Chinese white cabbage or pak choy) Separate the leaves and wash well before use. A smaller variety is known as Shanghai or baby bok choy — use it in the same way.

chinese rice wine

A fermented rice wine with a sweetish taste, similar to dry sherry. It is amber-coloured and is made from glutinous rice in Shaoxing in southern China.

fish sauce

A salty sauce with a strong fishy smell. Small fish are packed into wooden barrels, seasoned with salt and fermented for several months. The liquid run-off is fish sauce.

hoisin sauce

A thick, sweet-spicy Chinese sauce made from soy beans, garlic, sugar and spices. It is used in cooking and as a dipping sauce. Once opened, store in the refrigerator.

hokkien noodles

Thick, fresh egg noodles that have been cooked and lightly oiled before packaging. Often found vacuum-packed. Cover with boiling water for 1 minute to separate the noodles before draining and rinsing.

kecap manis

A thick, dark, sweet soy sauce often used in Indonesian and Malaysian cooking. If it is not available, simply stir a little soft brown sugar into regular soy sauce until it dissolves.

bok choy

fish sauce

hokkien noodle

Chinese rice wine

hoisin sauce

kecap man

lemon grass

An aromatic herb, best used fresh. Trim the base, remove the tough outer layers and finely chop the inner white layers. The whole stem can also be used in dishes such as curry, but remove it before serving.

mirin

A sweet spirit-based rice liquid used predominantly in Japanese cooking. Great in basting sauces and marinades, but also good in salad dressings and stir-fries.

oyster sauce

A thick, salty sauce made from dried oysters, used for both flavour and colour. Store in the refrigerator once opened. Vegetarian oyster sauce has a similar taste and is made using mushrooms as its flavour base instead of oysters.

palm sugar

A dark, unrefined sugar from the sap of sugar palm trees, sold in the form of dense, heavy cakes. Shave the sugar off the cake with a sharp knife. Comes in light and dark varieties.

sambal oelek

A hot paste made from fresh red chillies, chopped and mixed with sugar, salt and vinegar or tamarind. It can be used as a substitute for fresh chillies in most recipes and will keep, covered, in the refrigerator for months.

tamarind

A bean-like pod with a tart flavour. It is available as a dried shelled fruit, a block of compressed pulp, a purée or a concentrate. It adds a sweet–sour flavour to dishes.

lemon grass

oyster sauce

sambal oelek

mirin

palm sugar

tamarind

chinese beef and asparagus with oyster sauce

PREP TIME: 10 MINUTES + 15 MINUTES
  MARINATING
COOKING TIME: 10 MINUTES
SERVES 4

500 g (1 lb 2 oz) lean beef fillet, thinly
  sliced across the grain
1 tablespoon light soy sauce
1/2 teaspoon sesame oil
1 tablespoon Chinese rice wine
2 1/2 tablespoons vegetable oil
200 g (7 oz) fresh thin asparagus spears,
  cut into thirds on the diagonal
3 garlic cloves, crushed
2 teaspoons julienned fresh ginger
60 ml (1/4 cup) chicken stock
2–3 tablespoons oyster sauce

NUTRITION PER SERVE: Fat 16 g; Carbohydrate 4.5 g;
Protein 29 g; Dietary Fibre 1 g; Cholesterol 84 mg;
1200 kJ (285 Cal)

1 Place the beef slices in a large bowl with the soy sauce, sesame oil and 2 teaspoons of the rice wine. Cover and marinate for at least 15 minutes.

2 Heat a wok over high heat, add 1 tablespoon of the vegetable oil and swirl to coat the side of the wok. When the oil is hot but not smoking, add the asparagus and stir-fry for 1–2 minutes. Remove from the wok.

3 Add another tablespoon of oil to the wok and, when hot, add the beef in two batches, stir-frying each batch for 1–2 minutes, or until cooked. Remove the meat from the wok.

4 Add the remaining oil to the wok and, when hot, add the garlic and ginger and stir-fry for 1 minute, or until fragrant. Pour the stock, oyster sauce and remaining rice wine into the wok, bring to the boil and boil rapidly for 1–2 minutes, or until the sauce is slightly reduced. Return the beef and asparagus to the wok and stir-fry for a further minute, or until everything is heated through and coated in the sauce. Serve with steamed rice.

sesame chicken and shanghai noodle stir-fry

PREP TIME: 20 MINUTES
COOKING TIME: 15 MINUTES
SERVES 4

600 g (1 lb 5 oz) Shanghai noodles
1 tablespoon olive oil
1 tablespoon julienned fresh ginger
1 long red chilli, seeded and finely
  chopped
500 g (1 lb 2 oz) chicken breast fillets, cut
  crossways into 1 cm (1/2 inch) slices
2 garlic cloves, crushed
60 ml (1/4 cup) salt-reduced soy sauce
2 teaspoons sesame oil
700 g (1 lb 9 oz) baby bok choy, sliced
  lengthways into eighths
2 tablespoons sesame seeds, toasted

NUTRITION PER SERVE: Fat 19 g; Carbohydrate 80 g;
Protein 45 g; Dietary Fibre 6 g; Cholesterol 102 mg;
2850 kJ (680 Cal)

1 Cook the noodles in boiling water
for 4–5 minutes, or until tender. Drain,
rinse under cold water and drain again.

2 Heat the oil in a wok and swirl to
coat. Add the ginger and chilli and stir-
fry for 1 minute. Add the chicken and
stir-fry for a further 3–5 minutes, or
until browned and almost cooked.

3 Add the garlic and cook for a further
minute. Pour in the soy sauce and
sesame oil and toss to coat. Add the
bok choy and noodles to the wok and
stir-fry until the bok choy is tender and
the noodles are warmed through. Place
in individual serving bowls, sprinkle
with sesame seeds and serve.

*Pictured: sesame chicken and shanghai
noodle stir-fry*

singapore noodles

PREP TIME: 20 MINUTES + 30 MINUTES
    SOAKING + 30 MINUTES MARINATING
COOKING TIME: 10 MINUTES
SERVES 4–6

400 g (14 oz) dried rice vermicelli
60 ml (1/4 cup) soy sauce
60 ml (1/4 cup) oyster sauce
2 garlic cloves, crushed
2 teaspoons grated fresh ginger
250 g (9 oz) chicken breast fillets,
    thinly sliced
2 tablespoons oil
2 stalks celery, julienned
1 large carrot, julienned
3 spring onions (scallions), sliced on
    the diagonal
1 1/2 tablespoons Asian curry powder
1/2 teaspoon sesame oil
65 g (2 1/2 oz) bean sprouts

NUTRITION PER SERVE (6): Fat 12 g; Carbohydrate 20 g;
Protein 13 g; Dietary Fibre 2.5 g; Cholesterol 20 mg;
1003 kJ (240 Cal)

1 Soak the noodles in cold water for
30 minutes, or until soft. Drain well.

2 Combine 2 teaspoons soy sauce,
1 tablespoon oyster sauce, the garlic
and ginger, add the chicken and toss to
coat. Cover and chill for 30 minutes.

3 Heat a wok, add the oil and swirl to
coat. Cook the chicken, then add the
celery, carrot and half the spring onion,
and stir-fry for 2–3 minutes, or until
softened. Add the curry powder and
stir-fry for 2 minutes, or until aromatic.

4 Add the noodles, then stir in the
remaining ingredients. Serve hot.

chilli squid with hokkien noodles

PREP TIME: 25 MINUTES
COOKING TIME: 20 MINUTES
SERVES 4

500 g (1 lb 2 oz) hokkien (egg) noodles
750 g (1 lb 10 oz) cleaned small squid
    hoods
2 tablespoons lime juice
6 red Asian shallots
4 garlic cloves
2 small red chillies, chopped
2 coriander (cilantro) roots
2 stems lemon grass, white part
    only, chopped
1 tablespoon chopped fresh ginger
2 tablespoons tomato paste (tomato
    purée)
80 ml (1/3 cup) peanut oil
300 g (10 1/2 oz) baby bok choy
    (pak choi), chopped
2 1/2 tablespoons grated palm sugar, or
    soft brown sugar
1 tablespoon fish sauce
3 tablespoons coriander (cilantro) leaves
sliced red chilli, extra, to garnish

NUTRITION PER SERVE: Fat 15 g; Carbohydrate 42.5 g;
Protein 38.5 g; Dietary Fibre 5 g; Cholesterol 373 mg;
1940 kJ (460 Cal)

1 Cook the noodles in boiling wate for 1 minute, then gently separate Drain well.

2 Cut the squid hoods in hal lengthways. Score a shallow diamond pattern over the inside, being carefu not to cut all the way through. Cut into 5 cm (2 inch) triangles, then put in a bowl with the lime juice and refrigerate until needed.

3 Process the shallots, garlic, chilli coriander roots, lemon grass, ginge and tomato paste in a food processo until a fine paste forms.

4 Drain the squid. Heat a wok ove high heat, add 2 tablespoons oil and swirl to coat the side of the wok. Coo the squid in batches over medium hea for 2–3 minutes each batch, or unti tender. Remove from the wok. Cook the bok choy for 2 minutes, or until slightl wilted. Remove from the wok and add to the squid.

5 Heat the remaining oil in the wok add the tomato paste and cook stirring, over medium heat for abou 5 minutes, or until the oil separates Return the squid and bok choy to the wok, then add the hokkien noodles an combine. Stir in the palm sugar and fish sauce for 1 minute, then stir in the coriander. Garnish with the extra chil slices and serve immediately.

caramel pork and pumpkin stir-fry

PREP TIME: 15 MINUTES
COOKING TIME: 20 MINUTES
SERVES 4

250 g (1 1/4 cups) jasmine rice
300 g (10 1/2 oz) butternut pumpkin
  (squash)
500 g (1 lb 2 oz) pork fillet
2 garlic cloves, crushed
2–3 tablespoons peanut oil
60 g (1/3 cup) soft brown sugar
60 ml (1/4 cup) fish sauce
60 ml (1/4 cup) rice vinegar
2 tablespoons chopped coriander
  (cilantro) leaves
1.25 kg (2 lb 12 oz) mixed Asian greens
  (bok choy (pak choy), choy sum,
  gai larn)

NUTRITION PER SERVE: Fat 15.5 g; Carbohydrate 73 g; Protein 38 g; Dietary Fibre 6 g; Cholesterol 118.5 mg; 2445 kJ (585 Cal)

1 Bring a large saucepan of water to the boil. Add the rice and cook for 12 minutes, or until tender, stirring occasionally. Drain well.

2 Meanwhile, cut the pumpkin into pieces roughly 2 cm x 4 cm (3/4 inch x 1 1/2 inch) and 5 mm (1/4 inch) thick. Thinly slice the pork, then combine with the garlic and 2 teaspoons of the peanut oil. Season with salt and plenty of black pepper.

3 Heat a wok until very hot, add 1 tablespoon oil and swirl to coat. When just starting to smoke, stir-fry the pork in two batches for about 1 minute per batch, or until the meat changes colour. Transfer to a plate. Add the remaining oil to the wok and stir-fry the pumpkin for 4 minutes, or until tender but not falling apart. Remove and add to the pork.

4 Combine the sugar, fish sauce, rice vinegar and 1/2 cup (125 ml) water in the wok and boil for about 10 minutes, or until syrupy. Return the pork and pumpkin to the wok and stir for 1 minute, or until well coated and heated through. Stir in the coriander.

5 Place the mixed Asian greens in a paper-lined bamboo steamer over a wok of simmering water for 3 minutes, or until wilted. Serve immediately with the stir-fry and rice.

tofu, snow pea and mushroom stir-fry

PREP TIME: 10 MINUTES
COOKING TIME: 15 MINUTES
SERVES 4

250 g (1 1/4 cups) jasmine rice
60 ml (1/4 cup) peanut oil
600 g (1 lb 5 oz) firm tofu, drained,
    cut into 2 cm (3/4 inch) cubes
2 teaspoons sambal oelek or chilli paste
    (see Notes)
2 garlic cloves, finely chopped
400 g (14 oz) fresh Asian mushrooms,
    sliced (shiitake, oyster or black fungus)
300 g (10 1/2 oz) snow peas (mangetout),
    trimmed
60 ml (1/4 cup) kecap manis (see Notes)

NUTRITION PER SERVE: Fat 23.5 g; Carbohydrate 57 g;
Protein 29 g; Dietary Fibre 10 g; Cholesterol 0 mg;
2315 kJ (555 Cal)

1 Bring a large saucepan of water to the boil. Add the rice and cook for 12 minutes, or until tender, stirring occasionally. Drain well.

2 Meanwhile, heat a wok until very hot. Add 2 tablespoons of the oil and swirl to coat. Stir-fry the tofu in two batches on all sides for 2–3 minutes, or until lightly browned, then remove from the wok and transfer to a plate.

3 Pour the remaining oil into the wok, add the sambal oelek, garlic, Asian mushrooms, snow peas and 1 tablespoon water, and stir-fry for 1–2 minutes, or until the vegetables are almost cooked but still crunchy.

4 Return the tofu to the wok, add the kecap manis and stir-fry for another minute, or until heated through and combined. Serve with the rice.

notes Sambal oelek is made from mashed fresh red chillies mixed with salt and vinegar or tamarind.

Kecap manis is a thick sweet soy sauce available in the sauces or Asian food section of your local supermarket. If you can't find it, use soy sauce sweetened with some soft brown sugar.

variation You can use 3 teaspoons grated fresh ginger instead of the sambal oelek.

stir-fried beef and snow peas

PREP TIME: 10 MINUTES
COOKING TIME: 10 MINUTES
SERVES 4

2 tablespoons soy sauce
1/2 teaspoon grated fresh ginger
400 g (14 oz) lean beef fillet, thinly
    sliced across the grain
2 tablespoons peanut oil
200 g (7 oz) snow peas (mangetout),
    topped and tailed
1 small red capsicum (pepper), sliced
1 1/2 teaspoons cornflour (cornstarch)
125 ml (1/2 cup) beef stock
1 teaspoon soy sauce, extra
1/4 teaspoon sesame oil

NUTRITION PER SERVE: Fat 13 g; Carbohydrate 9 g;
Protein 27 g; Dietary Fibre 3 g; Cholesterol 67 mg;
1095 kJ (260 Cal)

1 Combine the soy sauce and ginger in a large bowl, add the beef and toss.

2 Heat a wok over high heat, add the oil and swirl to coat the side of the wok. Add the beef in two batches and stir-fry for 2 minutes each batch, or until the meat is golden. Return all the beef to the wok and add the snow peas and red capsicum. Stir-fry for a further 2 minutes.

3 Dissolve the cornflour in a little stock. Add the paste to the wok with the remaining stock, extra soy sauce and the sesame oil. Stir until the sauce boils and thickens. Serve with rice.

fried rice

PREP TIME: 10 MINUTES
COOKING TIME: 10 MINUTES
SERVES 4–6

60 ml (1/4 cup) peanut oil
2 eggs, beaten
220 g (8 oz) finely diced ham
100 g cooked prawns (shrimp), finely
    chopped
740 g (4 cups) cold cooked rice
40 g (1/4 cup) frozen peas
60 ml (1/4 cup) light soy sauce
6 spring onions (scallions), thinly sliced
    on the diagonal

NUTRITION PER SERVE (6): Fat 20 g; Carbohydrate 148 g;
Protein 30 g; Dietary Fibre 5 g; Cholesterol 110 mg;
3728 kJ (890 cal)

1 Heat a wok until very hot, add 1 tablespoon oil and swirl to coat. Add the egg and start to scramble. When almost cooked, remove the egg from the wok. Heat the remaining oil in the wok, add the ham and prawns, and toss to heat through evenly.

2 Add the rice and peas, toss and stir-fry for 3 minutes, or until the rice grains separate. Add the scrambled egg, sprinkle with the soy sauce and toss to coat the rice. Add the spring onion, stir-fry for 2 minutes and serve.

pictured: stir-fried beef and snow peas

satay chicken stir-fry

PREP TIME: 10 MINUTES
COOKING TIME: 20 MINUTES
SERVES 4

250 g (1 1/2 cups) jasmine rice
1 1/2 tablespoons peanut oil
6 spring onions (scallions), cut into 3 cm
    (1 1/4 inch) lengths
800 g (1 lb 12 oz) chicken breast fillets,
    thinly sliced on the diagonal
1–1 1/2 tablespoons Thai red curry paste
90 g (1/3 cup) crunchy peanut butter
270 ml (9 1/2 fl oz) coconut milk
2 teaspoons soft brown sugar
1 1/2 tablespoons lime juice

NUTRITION PER SERVE: Fat 46 g; Carbohydrate 57.5 g;
Protein 55 g; Dietary Fibre 5.5 g; Cholesterol 132 mg;
3600 kJ (860 Cal)

1 Bring a large saucepan of water to the boil. Add the rice and cook for 12 minutes, or until tender, stirring occasionally. Drain well.

2 Meanwhile, heat a wok until very hot, add 1 teaspoon of the peanut oil and swirl to coat the side of the wok. When hot, add the spring onion and stir-fry for 30 seconds, or until softened slightly. Remove from the wok. Add a little extra peanut oil to the wok as needed and stir-fry the chicken in three batches for about 1 minute per batch, or until the meat just changes colour. Remove from the wok.

3 Heat a little more oil in the wok, and stir-fry the red curry paste for 1 minute, or until fragrant. Add the peanut butter, coconut milk, sugar and 250 ml (1 cup) water and stir well. Bring the mixture to the boil and boil for 3–4 minutes, or until thickened and the oil starts to separate—reduce the heat slightly if the sauce spits at you. Return the chicken and the spring onion to the wok, stir well and cook for 2 minutes, or until heated through. Stir in the lime juice and season. Serve with the rice and a crisp green salad.

prawns with spicy tamarind sauce

PREP TIME: 15 MINUTES
COOKING TIME: 25 MINUTES
SERVES 4

80 g (1/2 cup) raw cashew nuts
250 g (1 1/4 cups) jasmine rice
2 garlic cloves, finely chopped
1 1/2 tablespoons fish sauce
1 tablespoon sambal oelek
1 tablespoon peanut oil
1 kg (2 lb 4 oz) raw medium prawns
   (shrimp), peeled and deveined with
   tails intact
2 teaspoons tamarind concentrate
1 1/2 tablespoons grated palm sugar or
   soft brown sugar
350 g (12 oz) choy sum, cut into 10 cm
   (4 inch) lengths

NUTRITION PER SERVE: Fat 14.5 g; Carbohydrate 60 g; Protein 35 g; Dietary Fibre 3.5 g; Cholesterol 186.5 mg; 2135 kJ (510 Cal)

1 Preheat the oven to 180°C (350°F/Gas 4). Spread the cashews on a baking tray and bake for 5–8 minutes, or until they become lightly golden—watch carefully, as they will burn easily.

2 Meanwhile, bring a large saucepan of water to the boil. Add the rice and cook for 12 minutes, or until tender, stirring occasionally. Drain well.

3 Place the garlic, fish sauce, sambal oelek and toasted cashews in a blender or food processor. Blend to a rough paste, adding up to 3 tablespoons of water, if needed.

4 Heat a wok until very hot, add the oil and swirl to coat. Add the prawns, toss for 1–2 minutes, or until starting to turn pink, then remove from the wok. Add the cashew paste and stir-fry for 1 minute, or until it starts to brown slightly. Add the tamarind, sugar and about 80 ml (1/3 cup) water, then bring to the boil, stirring well. Return the prawns to the wok and stir to coat. Cook for 2–3 minutes, or until the prawns are cooked through.

5 Place the choy sum in a paper-lined bamboo steamer and steam over a wok or saucepan of simmering water for 3 minutes, or until tender. Serve with the prawns and rice.

note To save time, you can purchase pre-peeled raw prawns with the tails intact. You will only need 500 g (1 lb 2 oz) as the shells make up roughly half the weight of the prawns.

squid with coriander, pepper and mung bean vermicelli

PREP TIME: 30 MINUTES + 5 MINUTES
  SOAKING
COOKING TIME: 10 MINUTES
SERVES 4

200 g (7 oz) mung bean vermicelli
2 garlic cloves, chopped
2 long red chillies, seeded and chopped
25 g (1/2 cup) chopped coriander (cilantro)
  stems and roots
1 teaspoon black peppercorns, dry roasted
  and crushed
2 tablespoons peanut oil
300 g (10 1/2 oz) cleaned baby squid tubes,
  scored and cut into 3 cm (1 1/4 inch)
  pieces
100 g (3 1/2 oz) asparagus spears, thinly
  sliced, leaving the tips whole
100 g (3 1/2 oz) sugar snap peas, trimmed
2 tablespoons fish sauce
1 tablespoon kecap manis
120 g (3/4 cup) roasted unsalted peanuts,
  roughly chopped (reserve 2 tablespoons,
  to garnish)
15 g (1/2 cup) coriander (cilantro) leaves
1 lime, cut into quarters

1 Place the vermicelli in a heatproof bowl, cover with boiling water and soak for 3–4 minutes, or until softened. Drain, rinse under cold water and drain again. Cut into 15 cm (6 inch) lengths.

2 Place the garlic, chilli, coriander, peppercorns and 1/2 teaspoon salt in a food processor or blender and process to a rough paste, adding a little water if necessary.

3 Heat the peanut oil in a wok over high heat. Add the paste and cook for 3 minutes, or until fragrant, then push to the side of the wok. Add the squid and quickly stir-fry until it curls, stirring in the paste to coat (it should not be in the wok for more than 1 minute). Remove.

4 Add the asparagus, sugar snap peas and 2 tablespoons water to the wok and stir-fry for 3 minutes, or until tender. Add the squid and the noodles and toss to combine. Stir in the fish sauce, kecap manis and peanuts.

5 To serve, divide among four serving bowls, top with the coriander leaves and reserved peanuts. Serve with wedges of lime.

NUTRITION PER SERVE: Fat 23.5 g; Carbohydrate 32 g;
Protein 22 g; Dietary Fibre 5.5 g; Cholesterol 149 mg;
1795 kJ (430 Cal)

shaking beef

PREP TIME: 15 MINUTES + 1 HOUR
          MARINATING
COOKING TIME: 10 MINUTES
SERVES 4

750 g (1 lb 10 oz) piece lean beef fillet
1¹/2 tablespoons fish sauce
1¹/2 tablespoons light soy sauce
1¹/2 teaspoons caster (superfine) sugar
6 garlic cloves, crushed
3 spring onions (scallions), white part only,
    finely chopped
60 ml (¹/4 cup) vegetable oil
2 teaspoons rice vinegar
2 teaspoons lime juice
1 teaspoon light soy sauce, extra
100 g (3¹/2 oz) mignonette or green oak
    lettuce leaves

NUTRITION PER SERVE: Fat 22 g; Carbohydrate 3.5 g;
Protein 41 g; Dietary Fibre 1.5 g; Cholesterol 126 mg;
1590 kJ (380 Cal)

1 Cut the beef fillet into 2 cm (³/4 inch) cubes and place in a non-metallic bowl. Combine the fish sauce, soy sauce, sugar, garlic, spring onion and 1 teaspoon of the oil in a small bowl or jug with ³/4 teaspoon freshly ground black pepper and ¹/2 teaspoon salt. Pour over the meat, toss together so that the meat is well coated, then cover with plastic wrap and refrigerate for at least 1 hour, or overnight.

2 To make the dressing, combine the rice vinegar, lime juice, extra soy sauce, 3 teaspoons of the oil and 2 teaspoons water in a small non-metallic bowl or jug. Wash, trim and dry the lettuce leaves, then toss with the dressing. Arrange the leaves on a serving plate.

3 Heat a wok over high heat, add 1 tablespoon of the oil and swirl to coat the side of the wok. When the oil is hot, add half the beef in one layer, allowing it to sit without stirring for 1 minute, so that a brown crust forms on the bottom. Stir-fry the beef quickly, or use the handle to shake the wok vigorously, tossing the beef around in the heat. Cook for 3–4 minutes for medium–rare, or until cooked to your liking. Remove from the wok and repeat with the remaining oil and beef. Arrange the beef over the lettuce leaves and serve immediately with steamed rice.

spicy noodles with pork and tofu

PREP TIME: 20 MINUTES
COOKING TIME: 15 MINUTES
SERVES 4

250 g (9 oz) hokkien (egg) noodles
1 tablespoon oil
500 g (1 lb 2 oz) pork fillet, thinly sliced
2 garlic cloves, crushed
2 cm x 2 cm ($^3/_4$ inch x $^3/_4$ inch) piece
    fresh ginger, julienned
100 g (3$^1/_2$ oz) snow peas (mangetout),
    sliced
100 g (3$^1/_2$ oz) fresh shiitake mushrooms,
    sliced
$^1/_2$ teaspoon five-spice powder
2 tablespoons hoisin sauce
2 tablespoons soy sauce
60 ml ($^1/_4$ cup) vegetable stock
200 g (7 oz) fried tofu, sliced
100 g (3$^1/_2$ oz) soy bean sprouts
fried red Asian shallot flakes, to garnish

NUTRITION PER SERVE: Fat 16 g; Carbohydrate 55 g;
Protein 45 g; Dietary Fibre 9.5 g; Cholesterol 75 mg;
2293 kJ (548 Cal)

1 Bring a large saucepan of water to the boil and cook the noodles for 2–3 minutes, or until they are tender. Drain well.

2 Heat a wok over high heat, add half the oil and swirl to coat the side of the wok. Add the pork in two batches and stir-fry for 2 minutes each batch, or until browned. Remove from the wok.

3 Add a little more oil if necessary, then add the garlic and ginger and stir-fry for 30 seconds, or until fragrant. Add the snow peas, mushrooms and five-spice powder and cook for another minute. Pour in the hoisin sauce, soy sauce and stock and cook, stirring constantly, for 1–2 minutes. Add the tofu, soy bean sprouts, noodles and pork and toss to warm through.

4 Serve immediately, garnished with the fried shallot flakes.

general tso's chicken

PREP TIME: 10 MINUTES + 1 HOUR
  MARINATING + 20 MINUTES SOAKING
COOKING TIME: 10 MINUTES
SERVES 4–6

Marinade

2 tablespoons dark soy sauce
2 tablespoons Chinese rice wine
2 teaspoons sesame oil
1 tablespoon cornflour (cornstarch)

900 g (2 lb) chicken thigh fillets
2 pieces dried citrus peel (2 cm x 3 cm/
  3/4 inch x 1 1/4 inch)
125 ml (1/2 cup) peanut oil
1 1/2–2 teaspoons chilli flakes
2 tablespoons finely chopped fresh ginger
120 g (1 cup) thinly sliced spring onions
  (scallions)
2 tablespoons dark soy sauce
2 teaspoons sugar
1 teaspoon sesame oil
thinly sliced spring onion (scallion),
  to garnish

NUTRITION PER SERVE (6): Fat 23 g; Carbohydrate 5 g;
Protein 27 g; Dietary Fibre 1 g; Cholesterol 119.5 mg;
1405 kJ (335 Cal)

1 Combine the marinade ingredients in a bowl. Trim the chicken of excess fat and sinew and cut into 3 cm (1 1/4 inch) cubes. Toss the chicken in the marinade, cover with plastic wrap and and marinate for 1 hour.

2 Meanwhile, soak the dried citrus peel in warm water for 20 minutes. Remove from the water and finely chop — you will need 1 1/2 teaspoons of chopped peel.

3 Heat the oil in a wok until it is very hot. Drain the chicken from the marinade using a slotted spoon and stir-fry the chicken in batches for 2 minutes, or until browned and just cooked through. Remove from the oil with a slotted spoon and leave to drain in a colander or sieve.

4 Drain all the oil from the wok except 1 tablespoon. Reheat the wok, then add the chilli flakes and ginger. Stir-fry for 10 seconds, then return the chicken to the wok. Add the spring onion, soy sauce, sugar, sesame oil, soaked citrus peel and 1/2 teaspoon salt and stir-fry for a further 2–3 minutes, or until everything is well combined and warmed through. Garnish with the spring onion, then serve with rice.

lamb, mint and chilli stir-fry

PREP TIME: 10 MINUTES
COOKING TIME: 15 MINUTES
SERVES 4

250 g (1 1/4 cups) jasmine rice
2 tablespoons oil
750 g (1 lb 10 oz) lamb backstrap (fillet),
  thinly sliced
2 garlic cloves, finely chopped
1 small red onion, cut into wedges
1 bird's eye chilli, finely chopped
60 ml (1/4 cup) lime juice
2 tablespoons sweet chilli sauce
2 tablespoons fish sauce
10 g (1/2 cup) mint leaves

NUTRITION PER SERVE: Fat 16.5 g; Carbohydrate 53 g;
Protein 44 g; Dietary Fibre 2 g; Cholesterol 122 mg;
2270 kJ (540 Cal)

1 Bring a large saucepan of water to the boil. Add the rice and cook for 12 minutes, or until tender, stirring occasionally. Drain well.

2 Meanwhile, heat a wok until very hot, add 1 tablespoon oil and swirl to coat. Add the lamb in batches and cook for 2 minutes, or until browned. Remove from the wok.

3 Heat the remaining oil in the wok, add the garlic and onion and stir-fry for 1 minute, then add the chilli and cook for 30 seconds. Return the lamb to the wok, then add the lime juice, sweet chilli sauce and fish sauce and stir-fry for 2 minutes over high heat. Stir in the mint and serve with the rice.

variation Try chicken breasts or pork loin, adding 80 g (1/2 cup) cashews and basil instead of mint.

teriyaki beef and soy bean stir-fry

PREP TIME: 15 MINUTES
COOKING TIME: 20 MINUTES
SERVES 4

400 g (14 oz) frozen soy beans
1 tablespoon peanut oil
700 g (1 lb 9 oz) centre cut rump steak,
    cut into 1 cm x 5 cm (1/2 inch x 2 inch)
    strips
6 spring onions (scallions), finely sliced
2 garlic cloves, chopped
2 teaspoons finely chopped fresh ginger
50 g (1 3/4 oz) soy bean sprouts
1 red capsicum (pepper), finely sliced
1 tablespoon mirin
2 tablespoons sake
2 tablespoons Japanese soy sauce
2 teaspoons sugar

NUTRITION PER SERVE: Fat 16 g; Carbohydrate 6.5 g; Protein 53 g; Dietary Fibre 6.5 g; Cholesterol 117 mg; 1590 kJ (380 Cal)

1 Blanch the soy beans in boiling water for 2 minutes. Drain well.

2 Heat a large wok until very hot. Add 2 teaspoons of the peanut oil and swirl to coat the side. Cook the beef in three batches for 3–4 minutes per batch, or until well browned. Remove from the wok and keep warm. Add the sliced spring onion and stir-fry for 30 seconds, or until wilted.

3 Return the beef to the wok, add the garlic, ginger, soy beans, soy bean sprouts and capsicum, and stir-fry for 2 minutes. Combine the mirin, sake, Japanese soy sauce and sugar. Add the sauce to the wok and stir-fry until everything is heated through. Serve with steamed rice.

notes Frozen soy beans are available in packets, either in their pods or shelled from Asian food stores. This recipe uses the shelled variety.

Traditionally, teriyaki refers to kebabs that have been marinated, grilled and basted with teriyaki sauce (mirin, sake, soy sauce and sugar). Alternatively, as in the above dish, the meat can be stir-fried, then simmered in teriyaki sauce until the sauce reduces to a glaze.

variation Chicken may be used instead of beef as a tasty alternative.

vietnamese caramel prawns

PREP TIME: 20 MINUTES
COOKING TIME: 10 MINUTES
SERVES 4–6

45 g (1/4 cup) grated light palm sugar
 or soft brown sugar
1.5 kg (3 lb 5 oz) raw medium prawns
 (shrimp), peeled and deveined
3 spring onions (scallions), finely chopped,
 white and greens separated
1 tablespoon vegetable oil
2 tablespoons fish sauce
1 tablespoon rice vinegar
2 garlic cloves, finely chopped
large pinch of white pepper
1 tablespoon grated light palm sugar
 or soft brown sugar, extra
1 tablespoon finely chopped coriander
 (cilantro) leaves (optional)

NUTRITION PER SERVE (6): Fat 4.5 g; Carbohydrate 10 g;
Protein 52 g; Dietary Fibre 1 g; Cholesterol 372.5 mg;
1215 kJ (290 Cal)

1 Put the grated palm sugar and 1 tablespoon water in a small saucepan over high heat and stir until the sugar dissolves. Bring to the boil and swirl the pan occasionally (but don't stir) for 3–4 minutes, or until it is dark golden and there is the first smell of toffee. Using a long-handled spoon, gradually stir in 60 ml (1/4 cup) water until a thin caramel sauce forms. Remove from the heat.

2 Combine the prawns and the white part of the spring onion.

3 Heat a wok to very hot, add the oil and swirl to coat. Add the prawn mixture and stir-fry for 1 minute, or until the prawns turn pink, then add the caramel sauce, fish sauce, rice vinegar, garlic, spring onion greens, pepper and extra palm sugar, and stir-fry for 2 minutes, or until the prawns are curled and glazed in the sauce. Toss in the coriander, if using. Serve with rice.

orange sweet potato, spinach and water chestnut stir-fry

PREP TIME: 15 MINUTES
COOKING TIME: 20 MINUTES
SERVES 4

300 g (1 1/2 cups) long-grain rice
500 g (1 lb 2 oz) orange sweet potato
1 tablespoon oil
2 garlic cloves, crushed
2 teaspoons sambal oelek
225 g (8 oz) water chestnuts, sliced
2 teaspoons grated palm sugar or soft
    brown sugar
390 g (13 1/2 oz) English spinach, stems
    removed
2 tablespoons soy sauce
2 tablespoons vegetable stock

NUTRITION PER SERVE: Fat 5.5 g; Carbohydrate 82 g; Protein 10.5 g; Dietary Fibre 6.5 g; Cholesterol 0 mg; 1785 kJ (425 Cal)

1 Bring a large saucepan of water to the boil. Add the rice to the boiling water and cook for 12 minutes, stirring occasionally. Drain well.

2 Meanwhile, cut the sweet potato into 1.5 cm x 1.5 cm (5/8 inch x 5/8 inch) cubes. Cook the sweet potato in a large saucepan of boiling water for 15 minutes, or until tender. Drain well.

3 Heat a wok until very hot, add the oil and swirl to coat. Stir-fry the garlic and sambal oelek for 1 minute, or until fragrant. Add the sweet potato and water chestnuts and stir-fry over high heat for 2 minutes. Reduce the heat to medium, add the palm sugar and cook for 2 minutes, or until the sugar has dissolved. Add the spinach, soy sauce and stock and toss until the spinach has just wilted. Serve with the rice.

chicken chow mein

PREP TIME: 15 MINUTES + 10 MINUTES
   MARINATING + 1 HOUR STANDING
COOKING TIME: 45 MINUTES
SERVES 4

250 g (9 oz) fresh thin egg noodles
2 teaspoons sesame oil
125 ml ($^1/_2$ cup) peanut oil
1 tablespoon Chinese rice wine
1$^1/_2$ tablespoons light soy sauce
3 teaspoons cornflour (cornstarch)
400 g (14 oz) chicken breast fillets,
   cut into thin strips
1 garlic clove, crushed
1 tablespoon finely chopped fresh ginger
100 g (3$^1/_2$ oz) sugar snap peas, trimmed
250 g (9 oz) Chinese cabbage, finely
   shredded
4 spring onions (scallions), cut into 2 cm
   ($^3/_4$ inch) lengths
100 ml (5 tablespoons) chicken stock
1$^1/_2$ tablespoons oyster sauce
100 g (3$^1/_2$ oz) bean sprouts, trimmed
1 small red chilli, seeded and julienned,
   to garnish (optional)

NUTRITION PER SERVE: Fat 39.5 g; Carbohydrate 39.5 g;
Protein 31 g; Dietary Fibre 4 g; Cholesterol 74 mg;
2685 kJ (640 Cal)

1 Cook the noodles in a saucepan of boiling water for 1 minute, or until tender. Drain well. Add the sesame oil and 1 tablespoon of the peanut oil and toss well. Place on a baking tray and spread out in a thin layer. Leave in a dry place for at least 1 hour.

2 Meanwhile, combine the rice wine, 1 tablespoon of the soy sauce and 1 teaspoon of the cornflour in a large bowl. Add the chicken and toss well. Cover with plastic wrap and marinate for 10 minutes.

3 Heat 1 tablespoon of the peanut oil in a small non-stick frying pan over high heat. Add one quarter of the noodles, shaping into a pancake. Reduce the heat to medium and cook for 4 minutes on each side, or until crisp and golden. Drain on crumpled paper towels and keep warm. Repeat with 3 tablespoons of the oil and the remaining noodles to make four noodle cakes in total.

4 Heat a wok over high heat, add the remaining peanut oil and swirl to coat the side of the wok. Stir-fry the garlic and ginger for 30 seconds. Add the chicken and stir-fry for 3–4 minutes, or until golden and tender. Add the sugar snap peas, shredded Chinese cabbage and spring onion and stir-fry for 2 minutes, or until the cabbage has wilted. Stir in the chicken stock, oyster sauce and bean sprouts, and bring the mixture to the boil.

5 Combine the remaining cornflour with 1–2 teaspoons cold water. Stir it into the wok with the remaining soy sauce and cook for 1–2 minutes, or until the sauce thickens.

6 To assemble, place a noodle cake on each serving plate, then spoon the chicken and vegetable mixture on top. Serve immediately, garnished with chilli, if desired.

vietnamese-style beef and bamboo shoots

PREP TIME: 10 MINUTES
COOKING TIME: 10 MINUTES
SERVES 4

60 ml (1/4 cup) vegetable oil

400 g (14 oz) lean beef fillet, thinly sliced across the grain

225 g (8 oz) sliced bamboo shoots, drained and rinsed

3 garlic cloves, crushed with 1/4 teaspoon salt

2 tablespoons fish sauce

3 spring onions (scallions), cut into 4 cm (1 1/2 inch) lengths on the diagonal

40 g (1/4 cup) sesame seeds, lightly toasted

NUTRITION PER SERVE: Fat 21 g; Carbohydrate 3 g; Protein 25 g; Dietary Fibre 3.5 g; Cholesterol 67 mg; 1275 kJ (305 Cal)

1 Heat a wok over high heat, add 2 tablespoons of the oil and swirl. When the oil is hot, add the beef in two batches and stir-fry for 1 minute, or until it starts to turn pink. Remove from the wok.

2 Add a little extra oil if necessary, then stir-fry the bamboo for 3 minutes, or until starting to brown. Add the garlic, fish sauce and 1/4 teaspoon salt and stir-fry for 2–3 minutes. Add the spring onion and stir-fry for 1 minute, or until starting to wilt. Return the beef to the wok, stir and cook for 1 minute, or until heated through. Remove from the heat, toss with the sesame seeds and serve with rice.

eggplant with hot bean sauce

PREP TIME: 20 MINUTES
COOKING TIME: 15 MINUTES
SERVES 4–6

60 ml (1/4 cup) peanut oil

800 g (1 lb 12 oz) eggplant (aubergine), cut into 2 cm (3/4 inch) cubes

4 spring onions (scallions), chopped

3 garlic cloves, crushed

1 tablespoon finely chopped fresh ginger

1 tablespoon hot bean paste

125 ml (1/2 cup) vegetable stock

60 ml (1/4 cup) Chinese rice wine

2 tablespoons rice vinegar

1 tablespoon tomato paste (tomato purée)

2 teaspoons soft brown sugar

2 tablespoons soy sauce

1 teaspoon cornflour (cornstarch) mixed with 1 tablespoon water

2 tablespoons shredded basil leaves

NUTRITION PER SERVE (6): Fat 10 g; Carbohydrate 5.5 g; Protein 2 g; Dietary Fibre 3.5 g; Cholesterol 0 mg; 550 kJ (130 Cal)

1 Heat a wok and add 1 tablespoon oil. Stir-fry the eggplant in batches for 3–4 minutes, or until browned. Remove.

2 Reheat the wok and add the remaining oil. Stir-fry the spring onion, garlic, ginger and bean paste for 30 seconds. Add the stock, rice wine, rice vinegar, tomato paste, sugar and soy, and stir-fry for 1 minute.

3 Add the cornflour paste to the wok and bring to the boil. Return the eggplant to the wok and stir-fry for 2–3 minutes. Serve sprinkled with basil.

phad thai with tofu, chicken and prawns

PREP TIME: 25 MINUTES + 10 MINUTES
    SOAKING
COOKING TIME: 10 MINUTES
SERVES 4

250 g (9 oz) dried wide rice stick noodles
2 tablespoons soy bean oil
3 garlic cloves, finely chopped
2 small red chillies, seeded and chopped
150 g (5^1/2 oz) chicken breast fillet,
    thinly sliced
200 g (7 oz) raw prawns (shrimp), peeled
    and deveined, tails intact
100 g (3^1/2 oz) fried tofu, julienned
    (see Note)
60 ml (^{1}/4 cup) fish sauce
60 ml (^{1}/4 cup) lime juice
3 teaspoons grated palm sugar or soft
    brown sugar
90 g (1 cup) soy bean sprouts, trimmed
45 g (^{1}/4 cup) unsalted roasted peanuts,
    chopped
3 tablespoons coriander (cilantro) leaves
lime wedges, to garnish

NUTRITION PER SERVE: Fat 20 g; Carbohydrate 20 g;
Protein 27 g; Dietary Fibre 4 g; Cholesterol 90 mg;
1505 kJ (360 Cal)

1 Soak the noodles in warm water for 10 minutes, or until soft. Drain.

2 Heat a large wok or frying pan until hot, add the oil and swirl to coat. Add the garlic, chilli and chicken and stir-fry for 2 minutes. Stir in the prawns and cook for a further 2 minutes. Add the noodles and tofu and toss until heated through.

3 Add the fish sauce, lime juice and sugar and gently toss until well combined and heated through.

4 Spoon the stir-fry onto a platter and sprinkle with the sprouts, peanuts and coriander leaves. Garnish with lime wedges.

note Fried tofu is a pre-cooked product found in Asian food stores.

pork with plum sauce and choy sum

PREP TIME: 10 MINUTES
COOKING TIME: 25 MINUTES
SERVES 4

600 g (1 lb 5 oz) choy sum, cut into
    6 cm (2¹/₂ inch) lengths

60 ml (¹/₄ cup) plum sauce

2 tablespoons Chinese rice wine

1¹/₂ tablespoons soy sauce

1 teaspoon sesame oil

125 ml (¹/₂ cup) peanut oil

1 large onion, sliced

3 garlic cloves, finely chopped

2 teaspoons finely chopped fresh ginger

500 g (1 lb 2 oz) pork loin fillet, thinly
    sliced across the grain

2 tablespoons cornflour (cornstarch),
    seasoned with salt and pepper

NUTRITION PER SERVE: Fat 33 g; Carbohydrate 18 g;
Protein 30 g; Dietary Fibre 3 g; Cholesterol 118.5 mg;
2070 kJ (495 Cal)

1 Bring a large saucepan of lightly salted water to the boil, add the choy sum and cook for 2–3 minutes, or until the stems are crisp but still tender. Plunge into iced water, then drain.

2 To make the stir-fry sauce, combine the plum sauce, rice wine, soy sauce and sesame oil in a small non-metallic bowl. Set aside until needed.

3 Heat a wok over high heat, add 1 tablespoon of the peanut oil and swirl to coat the side of the wok. Add the onion, garlic and ginger and stir-fry over medium heat for 3 minutes, or until softened. Remove from the wok.

4 Toss the pork in the seasoned cornflour to coat, shaking off any excess. Reheat the wok over high heat, add the remaining peanut oil and swirl to coat the side. Add the pork in batches and cook for 3 minutes each batch, or until golden on both sides. Remove from the wok.

5 Drain the oil and return the meat and any juices to the wok. Pour in the stir-fry sauce and cook over high heat for 2–3 minutes, then add the choy sum and the onion mixture. Cook, stirring, for a further 2 minutes. Serve immediately with rice.

ginger beef stir-fry

PREP TIME: 20 MINUTES + 15 MINUTES
  MARINATING
COOKING TIME: 15 MINUTES
SERVES 4

1 garlic clove, crushed
1 teaspoon grated fresh ginger
60 ml (1/4 cup) kecap manis
60 ml (1/4 cup) Chinese rice wine
1 teaspoon sugar
pinch of five-spice powder
500 g (1 lb 2 oz) beef fillet, cut into
  thin strips
1/2 teaspoon cornflour (cornstarch)
60 ml (1/4 cup) peanut oil
1 red onion, cut into thin wedges
1 1/2 tablespoons julienned fresh ginger
400 g (14 oz) gai larn (Chinese broccoli),
  cut into 6 cm (2 1/2 inch) lengths

NUTRITION PER SERVE: Fat 16.5 g; Carbohydrate 4.5 g;
Protein 27.5 g; Dietary Fibre 2 g; Cholesterol 83.5 mg;
1240 kJ (295 Cal)

1 Combine the garlic, grated ginger, kecap manis, rice wine, sugar and five-spice powder, add the beef strips and marinate for 15 minutes.

2 Mix the cornflour with 1 tablespoon water to form a paste.

3 Heat a wok over high heat, add 1 tablespoon of the oil and swirl to coat. When the oil is smoking, remove half the meat from the marinade with tongs or a slotted spoon, add to the wok and stir-fry for 2–3 minutes, or until browned and just cooked. Remove from the wok. Repeat with more oil and the remaining beef. Remove from the wok.

4 Add the remaining oil to the wok and stir-fry the onion for 2–3 minutes or until it starts to soften, then add the julienned ginger and stir-fry for another minute. Stir in the gai larn and cook for 2–3 minutes, or until wilted and tender.

5 Return the beef to the wok, along with the reserved marinade and any meat juices. Add the cornflour paste and stir to thoroughly combine. Continue to cook for 1–2 minutes, or until the sauce has thickened slightly and the meat is heated through. Serve with rice or noodles.

singapore pepper crab

PREP TIME: 15 MINUTES + 1 HOUR
  FREEZING
COOKING TIME: 20 MINUTES
SERVES 4

2 kg (4 lb 8 oz) blue swimmer crabs
4 tablespoons dark soy sauce
2 tablespoons oyster sauce
1 tablespoon grated palm sugar or
  soft brown sugar
1–2 tablespoons peanut oil
150 g (5 1/2 oz) butter
3 tablespoons finely chopped garlic
1 tablespoon finely chopped fresh ginger
1 small red chilli, seeded and finely
  chopped
1 1/2 tablespoons ground black pepper
  spring onion (scallion), green part only,
  thinly sliced on the diagonal

NUTRITION PER SERVE: Fat 12 g; Carbohydrate 20 g;
Protein 33 g; Dietary Fibre 3 g; Cholesterol 210 mg;
1310 kJ (313 Cal)

1 Wash the crabs well with a stiff brush. Pull back the apron and remove the top shell from each crab (it should come off easily and in one piece). Remove the intestine and the grey feathery gills. Using a large sharp knife, cut the crab lengthways through the centre of the body, to form two halves with the legs attached. Cut each half in half again, crossways. Crack the thicker part of the legs with the back of a heavy knife or crab crackers to allow the flavour to get into the meat and make it easier for your guests to break them open to access the crab meat.

2 Combine the soy sauce, oyster sauce and palm sugar in a small bowl.

3 Heat a wok to very hot, add 1 tablespoon of the oil and swirl to coat the side of the wok. When the oil is just starting to smoke, add the crab pieces in a few batches, stir-frying over very high heat for 4 minutes, or until the shells turn bright orange all over, using a little more oil if needed. Remove from the wok.

4 Reduce the heat to high, add the butter, garlic, ginger, chilli and pepper and stir-fry for 30 seconds, or until fragrant, then add the soy and oyster sauce mixture and simmer for a further minute, or until glossy.

5 Return the crab to the wok, cover, and cook, stirring every minute for 4 minutes, or until the crab is cooked through. Sprinkle with spring onion and serve immediately with rice, accompanied by small bowls of warm water to wash off sticky fingers.

notes   The seeds and membrane contribute most of the heat in chillies, so don't remove them if you prefer a spicier sauce.

This dish is very rich. In Singapore, this crab is served with paper bibs as it is very messy to eat — a paper towel or napkin will do just as well.

variation   You can use any variety of raw crab for this recipe.

mongolian lamb

PREP TIME: 25 MINUTES + OVERNIGHT
    MARINATING
COOKING TIME: 15 MINUTES
SERVES 4–6

1 kg (2 lb 4 oz) lamb loin fillets
    (e.g. backstraps or sirloin)
2 garlic cloves, crushed
2 teaspoons finely grated fresh ginger
60 ml ($1/4$ cup) Chinese rice wine
60 ml ($1/4$ cup) soy sauce
2 tablespoons hoisin sauce
1 teaspoon sesame oil
80 ml ($1/3$ cup) peanut oil
6 spring onions (scallions), cut into
    3 cm ($1^1/4$ inch) lengths
$1/2$ tablespoon chilli sauce
$1^1/2$ tablespoons hoisin sauce, extra

NUTRITION PER SERVE (6): Fat 26 g; Carbohydrate 6.5 g;
Protein 36.5 g; Dietary Fibre 2 g; Cholesterol 113.5 mg;
1745 kJ (415 Cal)

1 Cut the lamb across the grain into very thin slices. Place the garlic, ginger, Chinese rice wine, soy sauce, hoisin sauce and sesame oil in a large non metallic bowl and stir until well combined. Add the lamb and toss until it is well coated in the sauce. Cover and leave to marinate overnight, tossing occasionally.

2 Heat a wok over high heat, add 1 tablespoon of the peanut oil and swirl to coat the wok. Add the spring onion and stir-fry for 1 minute, or until lightly golden. Remove, reserving the oil in the wok.

3 Lift the lamb out of the marinade with tongs, reserving the marinade. Add the meat in four batches and stir-fry for 1–2 minutes per batch, or until browned but not completely cooked through, adding more oil and making sure the wok is very hot before cooking each batch. Return all the meat and any juices to the wok with the spring onion and stir-fry for 1 minute, or until meat is cooked through.

4 Remove the meat and spring onion from the wok with a slotted spoon and place in a serving bowl, retaining the liquid in the wok. Add any reserved marinade to the wok along with the chilli sauce and extra hoisin sauce, then boil for 3–4 minutes, or until the sauce thickens and becomes slightly syrupy. Spoon the sauce over the lamb, toss together well, then serve with steamed rice.

emon grass beef

PREP TIME: 15 MINUTES + 10 MINUTES
  MARINATING
COOKING TIME: 25 MINUTES
SERVES 4

00 g (1 1/2 cups) long-grain rice
  garlic cloves, finely chopped
  tablespoon grated fresh ginger
  stems lemon grass (white part only),
  finely chopped
1/2 tablespoons oil
00 g (1 lb 5 oz) lean rump steak, trimmed
  and cut thinly across the grain
  tablespoon lime juice
-2 tablespoons fish sauce
  tablespoons kecap manis
  large red onion, cut into small wedges
00 g (7 oz) green beans, cut on the
  diagonal into 5 cm (2 inch) lengths

NUTRITION PER SERVE: Fat 19 g; Carbohydrate 63 g;
otein 40 g; Dietary Fibre 3 g; Cholesterol 96 mg;
160 kJ (590 Cal)

1 Bring a large saucepan of water to the boil. Add the rice and cook for 12 minutes, or until tender, stirring occasionally. Drain well.

2 Meanwhile, combine the garlic, ginger, lemon grass and 2 teaspoons of the oil in a non-metallic bowl. Add the beef, then marinate for 10 minutes. Combine the lime juice, fish sauce and kecap manis.

3 Heat a wok until very hot, add 1 tablespoon oil and swirl to coat. Stir-fry the beef in batches for 2–3 minutes, or until it is browned. Remove from the wok.

4 Reheat the wok to very hot, heat the remaining oil, then add the onion and stir-fry for 2 minutes. Add the beans and cook for another 2 minutes, then return the beef to the wok. Pour in the fish sauce mixture and cook until heated through. Serve with the rice.

note Ensure your lemon grass is fresh — the end of the stalk should not be too dry and should still have a strong lemon scent.

ginger chicken stir-fry with hokkien noodles

PREP TIME: 15 MINUTES + 5 MINUTES
  SOAKING
COOKING TIME: 10 MINUTES
SERVES 4

2¹/₂ tablespoons finely shredded
  fresh ginger
60 ml (¹/₄ cup) mirin
2 tablespoons soy sauce
600 g (1 lb 5 oz) chicken tenderloins or
  chicken breast fillets, cut diagonally
  into thin strips
180 g (6 oz) baby corn
350 g (12 oz) choy sum
150 g (5¹/₂ oz) fresh oyster mushrooms
500 g (1 lb 2 oz) hokkien (egg) noodles
2 tablespoons oil
2 tablespoons oyster sauce

NUTRITION PER SERVE: Fat 19.5 g; Carbohydrate 77 g;
Protein 49 g; Dietary Fibre 7 g; Cholesterol 115 mg;
2925 kJ (700 Cal)

1 Combine the ginger, mirin and soy sauce in a bowl. Add the chicken, coat well, then leave to marinate while preparing the vegetables.

2 Cut the corn in half lengthways, trim the ends off the choy sum and cut into 6 cm (2¹/₂ inches) lengths. If the mushrooms are very large, cut them in half. Soak the noodles in boiling water for 5 minutes. Drain and refresh under cold running water.

3 Heat a wok until very hot, add 1 tablespoon of the oil and swirl to coat. Remove the chicken from the marinade with a slotted spoon and cook in two batches over very high heat for 2 minutes, or until brown and just cooked. Remove from the wok.

4 Add the remaining oil to the wok and stir-fry the mushrooms and corn for 1–2 minutes, or until just softened. Add the remaining marinade, bring to the boil, then add the chicken, choy sum and noodles. Stir in the oyster sauce and cook, tossing well, for 1–2 minutes, or until the choy sum has wilted slightly and the noodles are warmed through.

spring onion lamb

REP TIME: 10 MINUTES + 10 MINUTES
  MARINATING
OOKING TIME: 30 MINUTES
ERVES 4

00 g (1 lb 5 oz) lean lamb backstraps
  or fillets
tablespoon Chinese rice wine or
  dry sherry
) ml (1/4 cup) soy sauce
2 teaspoon white pepper
spring onions (scallions), cut on the
  diagonal into 4 cm (11/2 inch) pieces
00 g (11/2 cups) long-grain rice
tablespoons oil
50 g (1 lb 10 oz) choy sum, cut into
  10 cm (4 inch) lengths
garlic cloves, crushed
tablespoon Chinese black vinegar
teaspoon sesame oil

TRITION PER SERVE: Fat 19 g; Carbohydrate 63 g;
otein 38.5 g; Dietary Fibre 4 g; Cholesterol 100.5
; 2450 kJ (585 Cal)

Cut the lamb backstrap across the
ain into very thin slices. Place in a
owl with the rice wine, 1 tablespoon
 the soy sauce, 1/2 teaspoon salt and
e white pepper and mix well. Cover
d refrigerate for 10 minutes.

2 Meanwhile, bring a large saucepan of water to the boil. Add the rice and cook for 12 minutes, or until tender, stirring occasionally. Drain.

3 Heat a wok over high heat, add 1/2 tablespoon oil and swirl to coat. Add the choy sum, stir-fry quickly, then add 1 clove of garlic and 1 tablespoon soy sauce. Cook for 3 minutes, or until crisp. Immediately take the wok off the heat, remove the greens from the wok and keep warm.

4 Wipe the wok clean and heat over high heat, then add 1 tablespoon oil and swirl to coat. Add the lamb in two batches and stir-fry quickly over high heat for 1–2 minutes, or until brown. Remove from the wok.

5 Add a little more oil to the wok, if necessary. Add the spring onion and remaining garlic and stir-fry for 1–2 minutes. Combine the vinegar, sesame oil and the remaining soy sauce. Pour into the wok, stirring for 1 minute, or until combined. Return the lamb to the wok and continue to stir-fry for another minute, or until combined and heated through. Serve immediately with the stir-fried greens and rice.

note Chinese rice wine and Chinese black vinegar are available in Asian grocery stores.

asian greens with teriyaki tofu dressing

PREP TIME: 15 MINUTES
COOKING TIME: 20 MINUTES
SERVES 6

650 g (1 lb 7 oz) baby bok choy (pak choi)
500 g (1 lb 2 oz) choy sum
440 g (1 lb) snake beans, topped
    and tailed
60 ml ($^1/_4$ cup) oil
1 onion, thinly sliced
60 g ($^1/_3$ cup) soft brown sugar
$^1/_2$ teaspoon ground chilli
2 tablespoons grated fresh ginger
250 ml (1 cup) teriyaki sauce
1 tablespoon sesame oil
600 g (1 lb 5 oz) silken firm tofu, drained

NUTRITION PER SERVE: Fat 11 g; Carbohydrate 20 g;
Protein 19 g; Dietary Fibre 11 g; Cholesterol 1 mg;
1093 kJ (260 Cal)

1 Cut the bok choy and choy sum widthways into thirds. Cut the snake beans into 10 cm (4 inch) lengths.

2 Heat a wok over high heat, add 1 tablespoon of the oil and swirl to coat the side. Cook the onion in batches for 3–5 minutes, or until crisp. Remove with a slotted spoon and drain on paper towels.

3 Heat 1 tablespoon of the oil in the wok, add half the greens and stir-fry for 2–3 minutes, or until wilted. Remove and keep warm. Repeat with the remaining oil and greens. Remove. Drain any liquid from the wok.

4 Add the combined sugar, chilli, ginger and teriyaki sauce to the wok and bring to the boil. Simmer for 1 minute. Add the sesame oil and tofu and simmer for 2 minutes, turning once — the tofu will break up. Divide the greens among serving plates, then top with the dressing. Sprinkle with the fried onion.

warm citrus beef stir-fry

PREP TIME: 25 MINUTES
COOKING TIME: 15 MINUTES
SERVES 4

l, for cooking
00 g (1 lb 2 oz) rump or sirloin steak,
  cut into thin strips
onion, sliced
garlic cloves, crushed
teaspoon grated fresh ginger
teaspoon grated lemon zest
teaspoon grated orange zest
tablespoon lemon juice
tablespoon orange juice
00 g (3^1/$_2$ oz) rocket (arugula) leaves
0 g (1^1/$_2$ oz) snow pea sprouts
lemon, segmented
orange, segmented

NUTRITION PER SERVE: Fat 15 g; Carbohydrate 7 g;
otein 30 g; Dietary Fibre 3 g; Cholesterol 85 mg;
45 kJ (275 Cal)

Heat the wok until very hot, add
tablespoon of the oil and swirl it
round. Stir-fry the beef in small
atches until browned, adding more oil
necessary. Remove from the wok.

Reheat the wok, add 1 tablespoon
oil and stir-fry the onion, garlic and
nger for 3–4 minutes, or until tender.
eturn the meat to the wok along with
e combined citrus zest and juice.

Bring the liquid to the boil, then
ss the rocket through the beef
ixture and cook until the rocket is
st wilted. Serve on a bed of snow pea
routs, surrounded by the lemon and
ange segments.

sweet chilli squid

PREP TIME: 20 MINUTES
COOKING TIME: 10 MINUTES
SERVES 4

750 g (1 lb 10 oz) squid hoods
1 tablespoon peanut oil
1 tablespoon finely grated fresh ginger
2 garlic cloves, crushed
8 spring onions (scallions), chopped
2 tablespoons sweet chilli sauce
2 tablespoons Chinese barbecue sauce
1 tablespoon soy sauce
550 g (1 lb 4 oz) bok choy (pak choi),
    cut into 3 cm (1^1/$_4$ inch) pieces
1 tablespoon chopped coriander
    (cilantro) leaves

NUTRITION PER SERVE: Fat 8 g; Carbohydrate 4 g;
Protein 40 g; Dietary Fibre 7.5 g; Cholesterol 375 mg;
1030 kJ (245 Cal)

1 Cut the squid hoods open, score
diagonal slashes across the inside
surface without cutting right through
and cut into 2 cm x 9 cm (^{3}/$_4$ inch x
3^1/$_2$ inch) pieces.

2 Heat a wok until very hot, add the
oil and swirl to coat. Add the ginger,
garlic, spring onion and squid, and stir-
fry for 3 minutes, or until browned.

3 Add the sauces and 2 tablespoons
water to the wok, and stir-fry for
2 minutes, or until the squid is just
tender. Add the bok choy pieces and
coriander, and stir-fry for 1 minute, or
until the bok choy is tender.

ctured: warm citrus beef stir-fry

calamari in black bean and chilli sauce

PREP TIME: 20 MINUTES
COOKING TIME: 10 MINUTES
SERVES 4

4 squid hoods
2 tablespoons oil
1 onion, cut into 8 wedges
1 red capsicum (pepper), sliced
115 g (4 oz) baby corn, cut in halves
3 spring onions (scallions), cut into 3 cm
    (1 1/4 inch) lengths (optional)

Black bean and chilli sauce

3 teaspoons cornflour (cornstarch)
2 tablespoons canned salted black beans,
    washed and drained
2 small red chillies, seeded and chopped
2 garlic cloves, finely chopped
2 teaspoons grated fresh ginger
2 tablespoons oyster sauce
2 teaspoons soy sauce
1 teaspoon sugar

NUTRITION PER SERVE: Fat 10.5 g; Carbohydrate 12.5 g;
Protein 11.5 g; Dietary Fibre 4 g; Cholesterol 100 mg;
800 kJ (190 Cal)

1 Open out each squid hood. Score shallow diamond pattern over th inside surface of each, without cuttin right through, then cut the hoods int 5 cm (2 inch) squares.

2 For the sauce, mix the cornflou with 125 ml (1/2 cup) water in a sma bowl. Place the black beans in a bov and mash with a fork. Add the chill garlic, ginger, oyster and soy sauce sugar and the cornflour mix and stir.

3 Heat the oil in a wok or frying pa over high heat, add the onion and st for 1 minute. Add the capsicum an halved baby corn, and stir for anothe 2 minutes.

4 Add the squid to the wok and st for 1–2 minutes, until the flesh cur up. Add the sauce and bring to th boil, stirring constantly until the sauc thickens. Stir in the spring onio Serve with steamed rice noodles.

note Black beans are available fro Asian food stores.
variation Instead of squid, you can us fish, cuttlefish, prawns, octopus, or combination of the above.

index